First Facts®

Igloos and Inuit Life

the
BIG
PICTURE

CAPSTONE PRESS
a capstone imprint

Louise Spilsbury

First Facts is published by Capstone Press, a Capstone imprint,
151 Good Counsel Drive, P.O. Box 669, Mankato, Minnesota 56002.
www.capstonepub.com

First published in 2010 by A&C Black Publishers Limited, 36 Soho Square, London W1D 3QY
www.acblack.com
Copyright © A&C Black Ltd. 2010

Produced for A&C Black by Calcium. www.calciumcreative.co.uk

042010
005769ACS11

Library of Congress Cataloging-in-Publication Data
Spilsbury, Louise.
  Igloos and Inuit Life / by Louise Spilsbury.
     p. cm. — (First Facts, The big picture)
  Includes bibliographical references and index.
  ISBN 978-1-4296-5529-3 (library binding)
  ISBN 978-1-4296-5530-9 (paperback)
  1. Igloos—Juvenile literature. 2. Inuit—Dwellings—Juvenile
literature. I. Title. II. Series.

  E99.E7.S56 2011
  971.9004'9712—dc22   2010015735

Acknowledgements

The publishers would like to thank the following for their kind permission to reproduce their photographs:

Cover: Photolibrary: Radius Images (front), Shutterstock: Geoffrey Kuchera (back). **Pages:** Alamy Images: Picture
Contact/Ton Koene 20; Corbis: Wolfgang Kaehler 10; Fotolia: AlexQ 19, Michael Kempf 12-13, Tyler Olson 6-7;
Istockphoto: Michael Olson 4-5; Photolibrary: White Fox 9, 14-15; Rex Features: Martha Holmes/Nature Picture
Library 6-7; Shutterstock: Eyespeak 3, Geoffrey Kuchera 17, Laila R 4-5, 14-15, Tropinina Olga 12-13, Tyler Olson 1,
2-3, 8-9, 10-11, 16-17, 18-19, 20-21, 22-23, 24.

Contents

Igloos

Igloos are amazing houses built from just snow and ice. People called **Inuits** used to live in igloos.

Igloos today

Most Inuits do not live in igloos anymore. Today, igloos are mainly built for fun.

Snow place like home!

Warm inside

Igloos are built in places that are covered with snow and ice. But inside the igloo, it can be warm and cozy.

Igloos are strong. A man could stand on top of one without crushing it.

Build It Up

People can make an igloo anywhere there is snow that is hard enough to walk on.

Around and around

First, people cut thick blocks of snow. They put them in a circle. Then they put more blocks on top to build up the igloo.

Block by block

Igloos are built with thick, strong blocks of snow.

Keep out cold

When the igloo is built, people cover it with snow to stop the wind and rain from getting inside.

Look Inside

In the past, Inuits kept warm inside their igloos for most of the winter.

Light and heat

To light up the igloo, Inuits made candles from **seal blubber**. Candles also add some warmth.

Warm and cozy

Bedtime

At night, Inuits slept in sleeping bags.
They were made from **reindeer** skins.
The fur on the inside was warm and soft.

You can even have a fire inside an igloo.

Keep Warm

Igloos are cozy, but people still need to wear thick clothes to keep warm inside these homes.

Making clothes

In the past, Inuits made clothes from the skins of animals, such as bears and deer.

Inuits wear furry jackets called parkas.

Tough boots

Inuits made boots from seal skin. The skin is **waterproof**, so the boots kept out wet snow and ice.

I'm warm

Igloo Food

In places where people build igloos, it is too cold for many plants to grow. People who live here mainly eat meat.

Eat up

Inuits ate animals such as fish, whales, **walruses**, and seals. They ate their meat **raw**.

Inuits hunted walruses for their meat.

Keep it fresh

Inuits stored meat and fish by burying it in the ice. Then they covered it with rocks to stop animals from digging it up.

Freezing cold

On a Hunt

When they went on long hunting trips, Inuits built igloos to sleep in.

Clever fishing

Inuits sometimes built igloos on ice that covers the sea. They made holes in ice nearby to catch the fish swimming beneath.

Inuits fished with fishing rods made from animal bones.

Across water

Inuits used kayaks to travel across water to hunt sea animals. A kayak is a long, narrow boat.

Keep still!

In the Sun

When summer comes, the sun and warm weather melt igloos.

Summer living

In summer, Inuits lived in tents. Tents were made of seal or reindeer skins stretched over wooden frames.

It's melting

Busy days

Inuits used the summer to collect food such as wild berries. They stored the berries to eat in winter.

Reindeer skin was used for summer tents.

17

Getting Around

Inuits used dogs and **sleds** to travel in the past. Today they use high speed sleds to cross the snow.

Super sleds

Modern Inuit sleds are very fast and powerful. They are powered by a motor.

The sleds Inuits use today are called snowmobiles.

Zoom!

Tough dogs

Inuit sleds were pulled by husky dogs in the past. These are tough dogs that are able to survive in very cold places.

Today

Most Inuits now live in modern, heated houses. They buy their food from shops.

Remembering

Winters are long and cold where Inuit people live. To pass the time, they sometimes tell stories about what Inuit life was like in the past.

Life for young Inuits today is very different from the past.

Igloos today

Although most Inuits now live in modern houses, some Inuits still build igloos when they go on hunting trips.

Glossary

blubber thick fat from the body of an animal

Inuits people who live in northern Canada, Greenland, and the Arctic

raw not cooked

reindeer animal with long horns on its head; reindeers live in cold places

seal animal with flippers that lives on the land and in the water

sleds vehicles used to travel across snow

walruses animals with flippers and sharp tusks; walruses live on land and in the water in very cold places

waterproof keeps out water

Further Reading

FactHound offers a safe, fun way to find Internet sites related to this book. All of the sites on FactHound have been researched by our staff.

Here's all you do:

Visit www.facthound.com

FactHound will fetch the best sites for you!

Books

Living in the Arctic (Rookie Read-About Geography) by Allan Fowler, Children's Press (2000).

The Inside Story Igloo, by Dana Meachen Rau, Marshall Cavendish (2007).

The Inuit Thought of It: Amazing Arctic Innovations (We Thought of It) by Alootook Ipellie and David MacDonald, Annick Press (2007).

Index